Withdrawn

YOU CAN STOP BULLYING

STAND BY
OR
STAND UP?

You Choose the Ending

by Connie Colwell Miller • illustrated by Victoria Assanelli

Do you ever wish you could change a story or choose a different ending?

IN THESE BOOKS, YOU CAN!

Read along and when you see this:

WHAT HAPPENS NEXT?

Skip to the page for that choice, and see what happens.

In this story, Elizabeth sees Brooke bullying John. Will she stand up for John, or will she stand by? YOU make the choices!

Elizabeth is on her way to recess when she sees John and Brooke. "You're a loser, John," Brooke says. "You can't even throw a baseball!" Brooke shoves John. Elizabeth knows this is wrong.

WHAT HAPPENS NEXT?

→ If Elizabeth does nothing, turn the page.
If Elizabeth asks Brooke to stop, turn to page 20. ←

Brooke is a big and strong fifth grader. John and Elizabeth are only in second grade. Elizabeth doesn't want Brooke to pick on her too.

"Stop it," John says to Brooke. He tries to walk away, but Brooke grabs him by the arm and shoves him. "Where are you going, girly-boy?" she teases.

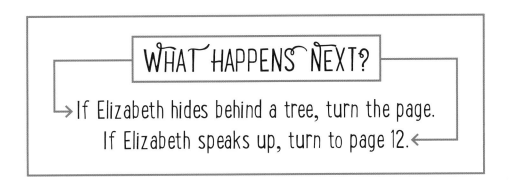

WHAT HAPPENS NEXT?

→ If Elizabeth hides behind a tree, turn the page.
If Elizabeth speaks up, turn to page 12. ←

"Let go of me!" John shouts. Then Brooke shoves John down. John's elbows scrape the ground and he begins to cry.

Elizabeth is scared of Brooke. She's not sure she can handle this problem on her own. Maybe she should get help.

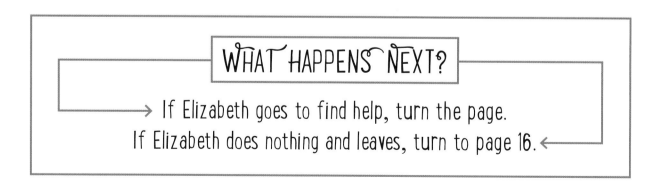

WHAT HAPPENS NEXT?

If Elizabeth goes to find help, turn the page.

If Elizabeth does nothing and leaves, turn to page 16.

Elizabeth wants to help John, but she wants to stay safe,
too. So she runs to find her friend Muna, a fourth grader.

A few minutes later, Elizabeth comes back with Muna. Brooke is still picking on John.

TURN THE PAGE $\rightarrow$

Elizabeth is less scared now. Muna is even taller than Brooke. Elizabeth and Muna walk up to John together.

Elizabeth says, "John, would you like to play baseball with us?"

John is relieved, and the three children go play together where they are all safe.

THE END

→ Go to page 23. ←

Elizabeth is afraid of Brooke. But she knows Brooke should not be shoving other people. She makes a difficult choice.

"Brooke!" she says. "Stop that right now!"

Brooke looks up, surprised. "Mind your own business, Elizabeth!" Brooke shouts.

 TURN THE PAGE →

Elizabeth knows she needs to go get help now. She runs to find an adult.

Mr. Payne, the recess aide, acts quickly. "Come with me immediately, Brooke!" he says.

Elizabeth helps John up and takes him inside to the nurse's office. She is glad she helped stop Brooke, but she wonders if John would have gotten hurt at all if she had stepped in sooner.

THE END

⤷ Go to page 23. ⤶

Elizabeth is scared. No one else is around to help her or John.

Elizabeth walks to the other side of the school where her friends are. She knows she'll be safe with more friends around.

TURN THE PAGE →

Elizabeth is playing with her friends when John walks by.
He is crying and his elbows are scraped up.

Elizabeth wishes she could have helped John.
She also worries that he will get bullied again.

THE END

→ Go to page 23. ←

Elizabeth doesn't want to make Brooke even more mad. But she knows what Brooke is doing isn't right.

"Don't talk to John that way," she says. "And no shoving!"

Brooke shrugs her shoulders and walks away. "Whatever," she says.

TURN THE PAGE →

"Thanks, Elizabeth," John says.

"Tomorrow, stick with a buddy on the playground," Elizabeth says to John. "And if Brooke bothers you again, find a teacher."

THE END

THINK AGAIN

- What happened at the end of the path you chose?

- Did you like that ending?

- Go back to page 3. Read the story again and pick different choices. How did the story change?

Bullying is everyone's problem—even those who are on the sidelines. If you saw bullying, how would you respond? Would YOU stand up, or stand by?

For the adorable Harper kids—C.C.M.

AMICUS ILLUSTRATED and AMICUS INK
are published by Amicus
P.O. Box 1329, Mankato, MN 56002
www.amicuspublishing.us

Library of Congress Cataloging-in-Publication Data
Names: Miller, Connie Colwell, 1976- author. | Assanelli, Victoria. 1984- author.
Title: You can stop bullying : stand by or stand up? / by Connie Colwell Miller : illustrated by Victoria Assanelli.
Description: Mankato, MN : Amicus Ink, [2020] | Series: Making good choices
Identifiers: LCCN 2018053332 (print) | LCCN 2018061132 (ebook) | ISBN 9781681517759 (eBook) | ISBN 9781681516936 (hardcover) | ISBN 9781681524795 (pbk.)
Subjects: LCSH: Bullying--Prevention--Juvenile literature. | Decision making in children--Juvenile literature. | Judgment in children--Juvenile literature.
Classification: LCC BF637.B85 (ebook) | LCC BF637.B85 M554 2020 (print) | DDC 302.34/3--dc23
LC record available at https://lccn.loc.gov/2018053332

Editor: Rebecca Glaser
Series Designer: Kathleen Petelinsek
Book Designer: Veronica Scott

Printed in the United States of America
HC 10 9 8 7 6 5 4 3 2
PB 10 9 8 7 6 5 4 3 2

ABOUT THE AUTHOR

Connie Colwell Miller is a writer, editor, and instructor who lives in Mankato, Minnesota, with her four children. She has written over 100 books for young children. She likes to tell stories to her kids to teach them important life lessons.

ABOUT THE ILLUSTRATOR

Victoria Assanelli was born during the autumn of 1984 in Buenos Aires, Argentina. She spent most of her childhood playing with her grandparents, reading books, and drawing doodles. She began working as an illustrator in 2007, and has illustrated several textbooks and storybooks since.